contents

Mr Jealous

CATHY WAS ROB'S NEW GIRLFRIEND LIKED HER A LOT.

That was a good day, Cathy. Thanks.

Yes, Rob. I had a good time too.

Cathy, am I your only boyfriend?

Oh no! I've got three! That's why I can only see you on Tuesdays and Thursdays!

Oh Rob! Don't be stupid! Yes, you *are* my only boyfriend.

Good! Listen, I'll phone you tomorrow.

OK.

BUT THAT WEEKEND, WHEN ROB SAW CATHY …

Well, Cathy. Did you have a good week?

Yes. I went to Tom's on Monday and Wednesday.

Oh yeah?

Learning Centres

Heart of Worcestershire College
Redditch Archer, Osprey House & Bromsgrove

Books should be returned or renewed on or before the last date below.

You can renew: In person at any Learning Centre
Renew by phone: **Osprey House**   **01905 725661** - All year round
                  Bromsgrove   **01527 572555** - Term time only
                  Redditch Archer   **01527 572519** - Term time only

Or e-mail us at :   renewals@howcollege.ac.uk

<table>
<tr><td></td><td></td><td>WITHDRAWN</td></tr>
<tr><td></td><td></td><td></td></tr>
</table>

Please note by borrowing this item
you are agreeing to abide by College policies,
including the payment of fines for late return.
NB: loss or damage to any item will be charged for.
FINES ARE CHARGED FOR LATE RETURN

221298 R

Addison Wesley Longman Limited
Edinburgh Gate, Harlow,
Essex CM20 2JE, England
and Associated Companies throughout the world.

ISBN 0 582 36368 3

First published 1999

Edited by Kate Robinson

Design by Neil Alexander
Printed in Spain by Mateu Cromo, S.A. Pinto (Madrid)

Published by Addison Wesley Longman Limited in association with Penguin Books Ltd, both companies being subsidiaries of Pearson Plc

Acknowledgements
Photostory photographs copyright © MG (My Guy) Monthly

Pages 14 and 16: Reproduced by courtesy of Images Colour Library;
Page 15: Reproduced by courtesy of The Image Bank/Antonio Rosario

She doesn't phone *me*, but she sees Tom every day! Is she playing a game with me?

She can't have two boyfriends. It's Tom or me.

I'll talk to her tomorrow.

BUT WHEN ROB TALKED TO CATHY, IT ALL WENT WRONG.

Cathy, who's Tom? Are you seeing him – or what?

Yes, Rob. I am. You know that.

But you see him every day now!

You're jealous, Rob!

I want you to see a photo of him.

Why?

I want you to see Tom. OK?

Roberto

SARAH'S DOING SOME WORK FOR HER SCHOOL EXAMS.

These exams are very important. I want to take some good photos of the river.

It's very difficult to understand this camera. I only want to take some photos. What's wrong with it?

Ah, I think it's OK now. Let's see.

Do you want to take a photo of me?

Hello!

OK then. Smile!

10

12

ALIEN
SPACECRAFT!

Alien spacecraft? 'No, never,' you say. 'There aren't any aliens.' But a lot of people here see spacecraft. Are they all wrong? What do *you* think?

THE DIAMOND OF LIGHT IN THE SKY

On the afternoon of 29 December, Betty Cash shut her shop in Crosby, Texas, and said to her two sons, Jack and Colby, 'Let's drive to Dayton. We can go to the cinema and eat at that new café.'

Ten minutes later, the two boys were in Betty's car. Jack was sixteen years old and Colby was eight.

Later that night, they drove back from Dayton. The small road was dark and quiet. They sang with the songs on the radio. Suddenly the radio stopped and there was a strong white light in the sky. It came down to ten metres over the road. 'It was a diamond of light,' Colby said later.

They opened the car doors and walked over to the light. 'It's dangerous!' Colby said. 'Let's go back to the car!' Betty went back to the car with Colby, but Jack stayed.

'Come back! It's dangerous!' Betty said from the car.

But Jack walked down the road. It was very hot near the light and he heard a lot of noises. The light did not move.

After five minutes, Jack went back to the car. He opened the door, and the door was very hot now. It burned his hand.

The three of them waited in the car. Ten minutes later the light started to move up into the sky. It was very quick. Then they saw two air force aeroplanes. The aeroplanes went after the light. 'I can't see,' Colby said. 'What did the aeroplanes do?' But Betty and Jack didn't want to get out of the car again to see.

They drove back to Crosby. Later they were all ill. Colby's face was burned and he had a pain in his eyes. Betty lost some hair. Jack was very ill. He saw a lot of doctors. He had a lot of pain in his head. His hands and arms and face were all burned.

They went to see important people in the air force. 'We saw two aeroplanes,' Betty said, 'over the road from Dayton to Crosby on the night of 29 December. There was a light in the sky. What did the aeroplanes do?'

But the air force people said, 'There were no aeroplanes there. There were no aeroplanes, do you understand?'

'But we *saw* the aeroplanes. And the light in the sky. Look at our faces – it burned us. Talk to us. Please ...'

What do you think? This was not one man or woman in the dark after some drinks. There were three people in the car that night. All three of them were ill. And doctors knew it too. What was the light in the sky? Was it a spacecraft? Where did it come from?

READING GAME

1 One evening you are in your garden. There is a light in the sky and then an alien spacecraft comes down near your house. Do you run away *(go to 2)*, or walk up to the space craft *(go to 3)*?

2 Do you go to the police *(go to 7)*, or do you go to get your family *(go to 4)*?

3 A door opens in the spacecraft. Do you run away *(go to 2)*, or wait *(go to 8)*, or walk into the spacecraft *(go to 5)*?

4 'Quick!' you say to your family. 'Come and see! There's an alien spacecraft in our garden!' They look at you, thinking 'Is this a game?', but they come and look. Now four people see the spacecraft *(go to 6)*.

5 The spacecraft moves up into the sky. You go with it. Your friends and family never see you again!

6 After five minutes, the spacecraft moves up into the sky. You feel sad. Did I lose a friend? you think. This is very important and exciting. I saw an alien. Aliens live in space – I know that now. They want us to be their friends. I will talk about this to people.

7 You talk to the police. 'There's a spacecraft in my garden!' you say. They look at you, thinking What?! Is this person ill? They go to your house, but now there's no spacecraft there. 'But I saw it,' you say quietly. 'I saw it.' You think 'Why did I run away?' Perhaps there were aliens in it. Now I'll never know.

8 A small alien walks from the spacecraft. It has two legs and two arms, but it is short and thin. Its eyes are very big and black, it has no nose and a thin little mouth. It looks at you and starts to talk. You don't understand, but you know it is friendly. It walks back into the spacecraft. Do you go with it into the spacecraft *(go to 5)*, or do you wait *(go to 6)*?

10 GOOD PLACES TO SEE SPACECRAFT

1 Alaska, 1986: people in a Japanese aeroplane saw a spacecraft in the sky. It stayed with the aeroplane for a long time, but then moved away.

2 Canada, Fort Resolution, 1995–6: lights moved in the sky over the town.

3 Norway, Hessdalen Valley, 1981–96: lights in the sky.

4 Russia, Voronezh, 1989: schoolchildren saw spaceships and tall aliens too.

5 China, Ghizhou Province, 1980: a lot of people saw a spacecraft.

6 New Zealand, North Island, 1978–9: lights in the sky; some people took photographs of these lights.

7 Australia, Rosedale, Victoria, 1980: people saw a large spacecraft.

8 Israel, 1985–9: a lot of people saw spaceships.

9 Zimbabwe, Bulawayo, 1985: a lot of people saw a spaceship. Two aeroplanes went after it, but it moved very quickly and the aeroplanes lost it.

10 USA, Hudson Valley, 1982–96: people saw 5,200 spacecraft in the sky!

Flowers for Maria

Herman looked up at the big white house. Maria took his hand and said: 'It's OK. He won't eat you.'

Her father met them at the door. He did not say hello. He looked at Herman coldly and walked into the house.

'Herman's a gardener, Daddy,' Maria said at the table.

'A gardener?' Her father's face went red.

'Yes, but I want to be a writer,' Herman said.

The father's eyes went black. He looked across the table at Herman and said: 'You writers are all thieves. You want my daughter because you want my money!'

'Daddy!' Maria said. 'You don't know him. Herman's not interested in money.'

'Good,' said her father, 'because he can't have mine!'

Herman stood up and looked sadly at Maria. 'I'm sorry,' he said. 'I can't stay here.'

And he walked out.

Two days later Herman wanted to say sorry to Maria. He went into a big shop and looked at some flowers. Maria will like these, he thought. He took some flowers and started to look for his money. But then he suddenly stopped. It was Maria! She was with her father, and they were in the flower shop! Oh no! Herman thought. I don't want to see *him* again.

He did not move. Maria and her father came very near, but they did not see him because of all the flowers. Herman wanted to run to Maria. He wanted to take her in his arms, away from her father. But this isn't a good time, he thought.

Very quietly, very slowly, he moved to the door. He watched Maria and her father all the time. Then, when he was near the door, he ran quickly into the street.

Suddenly he stopped. There was a hand on his arm.

'Come with me,' a policeman said.

'Why?'

The policeman looked at Herman's hands. Herman looked down too. In his hands were twelve beautiful red roses. 'No, please, you don't understand,' Herman said. 'I've got the money. I'm not a thief.'

But the policeman took him by the arm back into the shop, across the floor and to the boss's office. All the people in the shop watched him. Maria and her father watched him too.

'Herman,' Maria said, and she tried to run to him. But her father put his hand on her arm and stopped her.

'Now do you under-stand?' he said to his daughter. 'I was right. That man's a thief . Taking flowers from a shop because he doesn't have any money. You'll never see him again. Now come with me. I'll take you to lunch by the river.'

Maria did not want to go, but her father's hand was strong. 'All right, Daddy,' she said sadly. 'I'll come with you. But you're wrong about Herman. He isn't a thief. One day you'll understand.'

THE BULLY

SCHOOL STARTS AGAIN AFTER A TWO-WEEK HOLIDAY.

Good holiday, Bev?

Not bad, thanks. But now school again, same as always.

Oh no, there's Beverley.

And her friend Donna.

Let's go in now.

Look at Karen in that dress!

There's Beverley from B2. What a difficult girl.

And fat Gary, eating as usual.

We'll go in and talk to them. Ha, ha!

I don't like B2. They never listen to me and they aren't very friendly.

BEVERLEY IS INTERESTED IN THE NEW BOY.

YOSHI SITS WITH HIS NEW FRIENDS.

THEY WANT YOSHI TO BE QUIET.

Shhh!

Why are they all frightened of her?

THE FRIENDS TALK TO YOSHI ABOUT BEVERLEY.

SHE OFTEN TAKES GARY'S LUNCHBOX.

Give me your lunch!

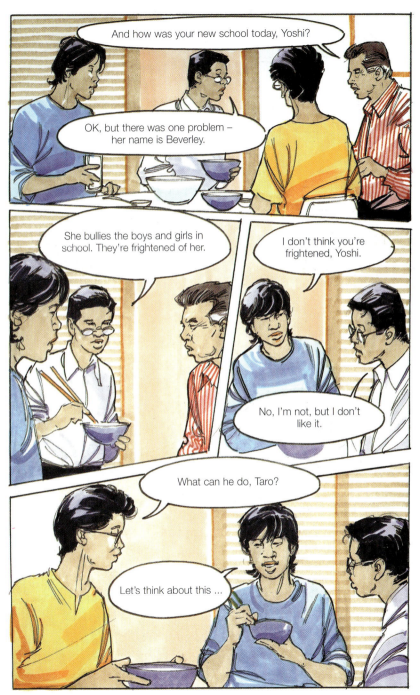

I know the answer – they can do karate. Ask them to come with us!

YOSHI SAYS THAT KARATE IS THE ANSWER TO THE PROBLEM.

That's good. I'll talk to them about it.

Good one, Yoshi!

You can do karate if you're small or big. I'm not strong, but I can do it.

I don't think Beverley knows karate.

It's important to think that you *can* do this.

EXIT

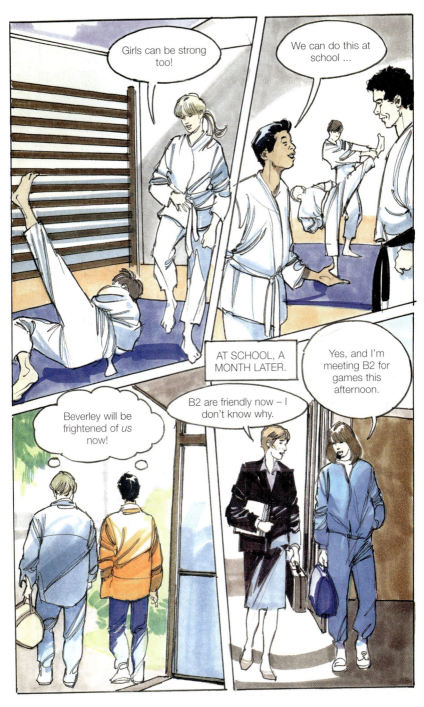

2

EXERCISES

Mr Jealous, Roberto and Alien Spacecraft!

Before you read

1   Find these words in your dictionary.

aliens   look after   students   camera   burned
stupid   diamond   exams   light   films   air force
pain   spacecraft   planet   person

Which words will you find in *Alien Spacecraft!?*

2   Put the words in these sentences:
a) She broke my _____ because she didn't _____ it. Now I can't take any photos.
b) _____ do a lot of work because they often have difficult _____.
c) Why don't you want to work for your school _____? That's _____!
d) A _____ in the _____ often goes in a plane.
e) We think _____ usually come in a _____ to see our _____.
f) It was very dark because there was no _____.
g) I had a lot of _____ in my hand after I _____ it.
h) I like going to see _____ at the cinema with my friends.
i) ◆ This is a _____.

3   Are *you* jealous of people sometimes? Why? How can you stop a friend from being jealous of you? What can you say?

After you read

4   In *Mr Jealous*, why is Rob jealous of Tom?
5   Do *you* think Rob is stupid?
6   In *Roberto*, why can't Sarah work the camera when she's with Roberto?
7   Do you like going to the cinema? Which films do you like, and why?
8   In *Alien Spacecraft!* what did the spacecraft do to Jack's face and hands?
9   Why did the air force people say 'There were no aeroplanes'?

Writing

10   You are Roberto, in Italy. Write a letter to Sarah in England. Tell her about your family, your friends, your school. And tell her you love her!

Flowers for Maria and *The Bully*

Before you read

11 Find these words in your dictionary.
   frightened   *thieves*   *bully*   *flowers*   *karate*
   problem
   Write sentences with the words.

12 Your friend's mother or father says to you 'I don't like you.' What can you do or say?

13 What can you do to stop a bully in your school?

After you read

14 In *Flowers for Maria*, why did Herman try to get out of the shop quietly?

15 Maria's father says: 'You'll never see him again.'
   Do you think he is right to say that to his daughter?
   Do you think she will see Herman again?

16 In *The Bully*, why is Beverley interested in the new boy?

17 Who first thinks of doing karate to stop Beverley being a bully?

Writing

18 You are Herman. You want to see Maria again, but perhaps she thinks you are a thief. Write her a letter.